The Memory Man

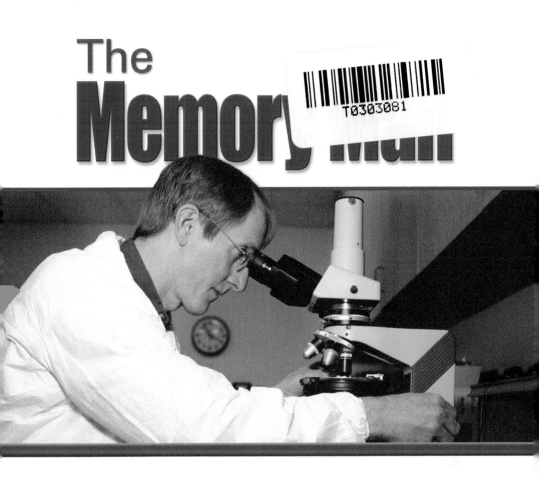

T0303081

Rob Waring, *Series Editor*

NATIONAL
GEOGRAPHIC
LEARNING

Australia · Brazil · Mexico · Singapore · United Kingdom · United States

Words to Know

This story is set in Europe. It happens in the country of Italy.

ITALY

EUROPE
ITALY
AFRICA

N
W—E
S

(A) **Environment or Family?** Read the paragraph. Use the correct form of the underlined words to complete the sentences.

Gianni Golfera [dʒɑni gɔlferə] has a very good memory. He can remember a lot of information. The capacity of his mind is so big that many scientists want to study it. Some think his good memory is because of his environment. They think his actions and the things around him improved his memory. Other scientists think that Gianni got his good memory from his parents' genes. They think memory characteristics come from the DNA of family members.

1. A _____ is a part of DNA that controls a certain characteristic.

2. _____ is the ability to remember.

3. The amount that something can contain is its _____.

4. Your _____ is the situation that you live in; what's around you.

gene

DNA strand

B Memory and the Brain. Look at the pictures and read the paragraph. Then match each word with the correct definition.

Dr. Malgaroli [mælgərʊli] is a kind of scientist called a neurobiologist. He studies the human brain and the nerves connected to it. In this story, Dr. Malgaroli studies Gianni Golfera to find out why he has a good memory. He thinks the answer may be in a part of the brain called the hippocampus. Researchers have studied the hippocampus. They have found that it is important in adding information to our memories. In it, information is coded, or recorded, in the brain.

1. neurobiologist _____

2. brain _____

3. hippocampus _____

4. researcher _____

5. code _____

a. someone who studies a subject in detail

b. a scientist who studies the brain and the nervous system

c. change information so that it can be stored

d. part of the brain which has to do with memory

e. organ in the head that controls thought, feeling, and movement

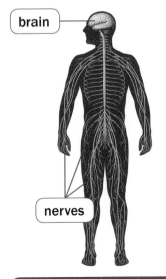

brain

nerves

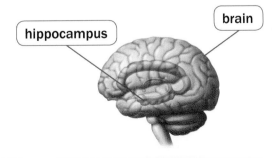

hippocampus

brain

The Human Nervous System — **The Brain and the Hippocampus**

Gianni Golfera is in front of a group of people. He's **blindfolded**,[1] but he can still show these people something that's amazing. The young Italian man calls it 'the art of memory.' First, the people who are watching him **randomly**[2] choose sixty numbers. After that, a helper reads the numbers to Gianni. Then, after hearing them just a single time, Gianni repeats the numbers in the correct order from memory. He does this first in the order he heard them. Then, he does it again—backwards!

---

[1] **blindfolded:** wearing something over the eyes so one cannot see
[2] **random:** done or chosen without any plan or system

 CD 3, Track 07

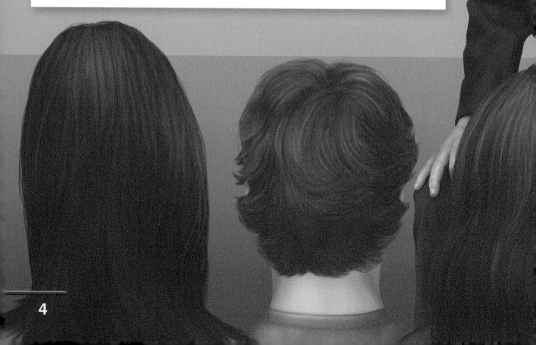

Gianni Golfera can remember long lists of numbers—forwards and backwards!

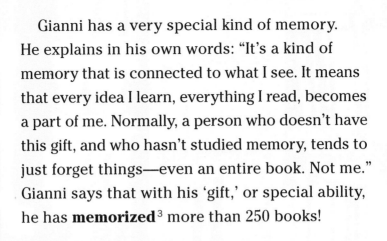

Gianni has a very special kind of memory. He explains in his own words: "It's a kind of memory that is connected to what I see. It means that every idea I learn, everything I read, becomes a part of me. Normally, a person who doesn't have this gift, and who hasn't studied memory, tends to just forget things—even an entire book. Not me." Gianni says that with his 'gift,' or special ability, he has **memorized**[3] more than 250 books!

Memorizing over 250 books is surprising, but it's not the only surprising thing about Gianni. He says that he can remember every detail of every day of his life. He also says that he can remember these details from the time he was less than one year old!

---

[3]**memorize:** learn something so that one can remember it exactly

Memory is very difficult to understand. Scientists don't really know how it works, yet. The Golfera family genes may hold important information about Gianni's memory. Neurobiologist Dr. Antonio Malgaroli plans to compare the Golfera family's genes with the genes of more forgetful families.

"The **crucial**[4] question," says Dr. Malgaroli, "is to understand which is the contribution from **heredity**,[5] and which is the contribution that comes from the environment."

---

[4] **crucial:** very important
[5] **heredity:** the passing of genes from parent to child

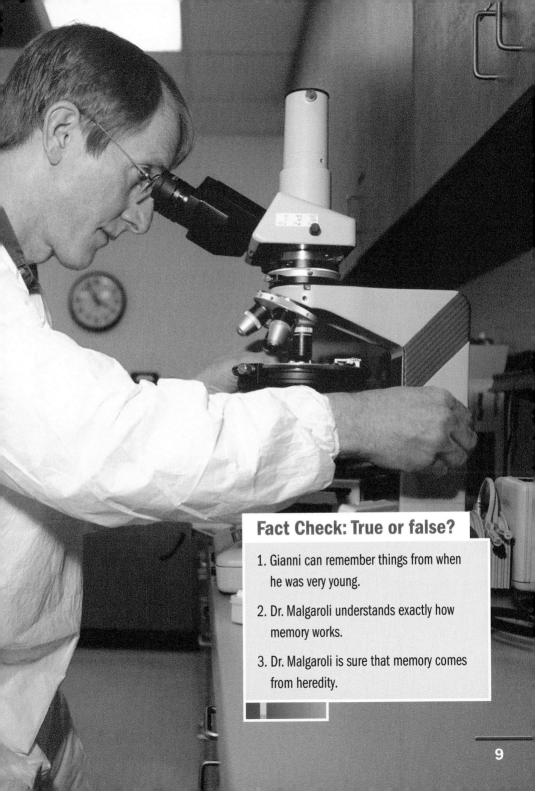

Fact Check: True or false?

1. Gianni can remember things from when he was very young.

2. Dr. Malgaroli understands exactly how memory works.

3. Dr. Malgaroli is sure that memory comes from heredity.

When we process new information, such as reading a book or newspaper, it goes into our brains. It gets into the brain through the part called the hippocampus. There, it's coded as memory. However, the actual process is still mostly unknown. How is memory coded? Where is it stored? Why is it stored there? These are all questions that are still unanswered. Nobody knows why or how these things happen. Nobody knows why some people lose their memories. They also don't know why so very few people are like Gianni and never forget things.

INFORMATI

book

Nobody knows how memory is coded in the hippocampus.

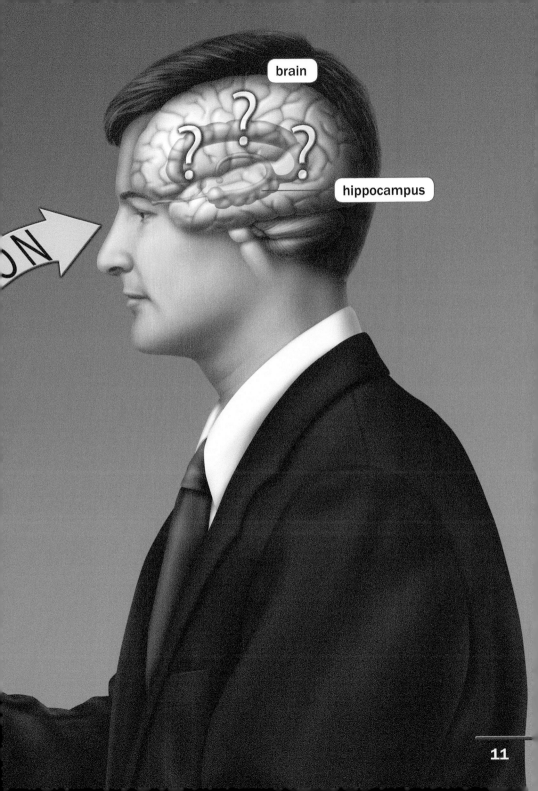

Researchers are now studying how memory and learning change the brain. They are also trying to match those changes to specific genes. They want to find out which memory characteristics are related to genes.

Some research already shows that a great memory may not depend on the right DNA only. It seems that everyone can remember more if they try. According to Dr. Malgaroli, "If you really need to use your brain capacity to store some kind of information, you have this ability. It's just a matter of exercise." Apparently, practice and exercising the brain can improve the memory!

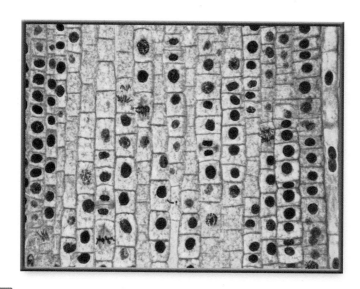

Identify the Main Idea

1. What is the main idea of Dr. Malgaroli's comment on page 12?

2. How does he think we can all improve our memories?

The same idea is true for Gianni. His genes are only part of the story. Since the age of 11, he's been training his brain to remember more and more. He practices continuously to improve the power of his memory. Gianni thinks about memory, and works on it, all the time. He has even memorized a whole series of historical books!

For Gianni, improving his memory has become almost like a full-time job. Dr. Malgaroli comments, "Golfera has an **extraordinary**[6] ability. The question is...how much it's really because of the Golfera family genes, and how much comes from his sort of '**maniac**'[7] type of activity."

---

[6]**extraordinary:** very special, unusual, or strange
[7]**maniac:** *(unusual use)* a person who spends most of their time on an activity of heavy interest

Gianni 's life is not all about science, though. He has a relatively normal life. He has a dog and a girlfriend. He likes to take time away from work. In other words, he's just like other people, and that's part of what's so interesting about him. Gianni's genes may be partly responsible for his great memory. However, researchers think Gianni's memory is mainly because of his very hard work. Gianni agrees. He believes that anyone can do what he does.

Gianni even offers proof that anyone can have a great memory. He holds classes to teach others how to improve their memories. His system basically involves organization and hard work. In his classes, Gianni shows people how to organize their memories and how to 'remember to remember.' Gianni explains: "I think the only problem with memory is the correct order. There's a lot of brain space, so I think there are no limits."

If there is a memory gene, Gianni Golfera probably has it. But the success of 'The Memory Man' may be more about **determination**[8] than DNA. Gianni's practice and hard work are making his very good memory even better. At the same time, he might just be showing scientists that a great memory can be made and not just born!

---

[8]**determination:** continuing to try to do something, although it's very difficult

After You Read

1. What is Gianni doing in the classroom on page 4?
   A. learning about memory
   B. showing his ability to remember
   C. choosing sixty numbers
   D. helping read the numbers

2. On page 4, 'them' refers to:
   A. people
   B. Italians
   C. helpers
   D. numbers

3. What is NOT a good heading for page 7?
   A. Gianni Isn't Connected to World
   B. Man Never Forgets
   C. Young Italian Has Gift
   D. Memory Man Is Special

4. In paragraph 1 on page 7, Gianni _____ that every idea becomes a part of him.
   A. proves
   B. demonstrates
   C. says
   D. agrees

5. In paragraph 1 on page 8, the phrase 'more forgetful families' means:
   A. families who can't remember as well as Golfera's
   B. more families in general
   C. families who can't forget things
   D. families who have good memory genes

6. On page 8, where does Dr. Malgaroli think good memory comes from?
   A. family
   B. environment
   C. heredity
   D. He doesn't know.

7. On page 10, 'it' in 'it's coded' is referring to:
   A. memory
   B. new information
   C. old information
   D. brain

8. Exercising our brains can help us to remember _____.
   A. less
   B. much
   C. more
   D. often

9. Which of the following does Gianni NOT do to train his memory?
   A. He works a full-time job.
   B. He practices a lot.
   C. He thinks about memory.
   D. He memorizes books.

10. On page 17, the word 'relatively' means:
   A. strangely
   B. fairly
   C. totally
   D. oddly

11. Which of the following describes Gianni?
   A. He only reads about memory.
   B. He loves his job.
   C. He is a great scientist.
   D. He tries to lead a regular life.

12. What does the writer probably think about having a great memory like Gianni?
   A. Anyone can do it with a little work.
   B. Italian people have a special gene.
   C. Heredity and practice both help memory.
   D. Memory is determined by family.

How to Improve Your Memory

We still have a lot to learn about how memory works, but scientists do agree on certain ideas. Neurobiologists know that we store information in three memory systems in our brains. They also know that we process this information in three different ways. The following charts explain these systems and processes.

Process	Definition	How It's Done
Encoding	putting information into memory storage	• *the brain notices and remembers what something means, how it sounds, or how it looks*
Storage	keeping information in memory storage	• *information is looked at again and again* • *similar ideas are grouped together*
Retrieval	getting information from memory storage	• *an existing thought is used to find an old idea that is stored in the brain*

Information Processes of the Brain

Memory Systems of the Brain

Memory System	Information Source	Time Stored
Sensory Memory	the senses: eyes, ears, etc.	*12 to 30 seconds*
Short-Term Memory	sensory memory storage	*several minutes or hours*
Long-Term Memory	short-term memory storage	*many years*

Now that you understand how the brain works, here are three simple suggestions from brain researchers to improve your memory:

1. CHOOSE CAREFULLY

Don't try to remember everything. Decide what it is that you really need to remember. Then spend your time studying this key information. Don't let yourself think about unimportant information and ideas, even if you find them really interesting.

2. TRY SOMETHING NEW

The brain learns more when we keep it active. It gets stronger when it is given something new and unusual to learn. If you are a swimmer, learn how to play soccer. If you speak English, learn how to speak Spanish. Learning a new language is a great way to keep your brain active.

3. GET ENOUGH SLEEP

The brain needs sleep and rest. While you are sleeping, the brain organizes all the information that it processed during the day. If you don't get enough sleep, the information is not correctly stored. It is then difficult to remember things the next day, especially if you are very tired.

CD 3, Track 08

Word Count: 332
Time: _____

Vocabulary List

blindfolded (4)
brain (3, 10, 11, 12, 14, 18)
capacity (2, 12)
code (3, 10)
crucial (8)
determination (18)
environment (2, 8)
extraordinary (14)
gene (2, 8, 12, 14, 17, 18)
heredity (8, 9)
hippocampus (3, 10, 11)
maniac (14)
memorize (7, 14)
memory (2, 3, 4, 7, 8, 9, 10, 12, 13, 14, 17, 18)
neurobiologist (3, 8)
random (4)
researcher (3, 12, 17)